Volume 66 of the Yale Series of Younger Poets

LUGGING VEGETABLES TO NANTUCKET

by Peter Klappert

New Haven and London

Yale University Press

Designed by Sally Sullivan
and set in Times Roman type.
Printed in the United States of America by
The Carl Purington Rollins Printing-Office
of the Yale University Press.

Published in Great Britain, Europe, and Africa by
Yale University Press, Ltd., London.
Distributed in Canada by McGill-Queen's University Press, Montreal;
in Latin America by Kaiman & Polon, Inc., New York City;
in India by UBS Publishers' Distributors Pvt., Ltd., Delhi;
in Japan by John Weatherhill, Inc., Tokyo.

Acknowledgment is made to the following publications for poems or versions of poems which originally appeared in them.
Armadillo: Four X-Love Poems (as part of "Five X-Love Poems"). / *The Atlantic Monthly:* Mail at Your New Address (part I). / *The Daily Iowan:* Skrophodupolos Honored by Reception (as "Poet Honored by Reception"). / *Epoch:* Pieces of the One and a Half Legged Man (revised from *The Trojan Horse);* Poem for L. C. (as "For L. C." and "Second Poem for L. C."); The Locust Trees. / *Epos:* Photographs of Ogunquit. / *The Greenfield Review:* A Man I Knew; Some People Are Never Satisfied (revised from *Poetry Venture*). / *The Iowa Review:* On a Beach in Southern Connecticut. / *The Massachusetts Review:* Instructions from the Dean of Menopause; Lugging Vegetables to Nantucket. / *The Nation:* Mail at Your New Address (part II, as "Happiness Is Mail at Your New Address"). / *New American Review:* Thanksgiving (as "Thanksgiving 1967"). / *The New Yorker:* The Invention of the Telephone. / *The North American Review:* Ellie Mae Leaves in a Hurry; In Memory of H. F.; Rowayton at 4 P.M. / *Poetry Venture:* Some People Are Never Satisfied. / *The Trojan Horse:* Pieces of the One and a Half Legged Man.
    The author wishes to thank the Faculty Research Council of Rollins College for two grants which made possible the writing of some poems in this book.

For Matt, Ülle,

and for the babysitters

How, if some day or night, a demon
were to come upon you
in your loneliest of lonelies

and say, "This life as you now live it
and you have lived it
you must live again and distant times

again, and there will be nothing new
but every pain
and every joy and every thought

must return to you, all in the same
succession, even
this spider-web, even this moonlight

even this moment and I myself.
The eternal hour-
glass of existence is turned over

and over, and you with it, dust
of a grain of dust."
If this thought possessed you, it would change you

as you are, or perhaps crush you.

—Adaptation from Nietzsche's *Die*
Fröhliche Wissenschaft, after a
translation by Walter Kaufmann

CONTENTS

FOREWORD

Peter Klappert is such a recklessly clever poet that one's first inclination is to mistrust his seriousness. His wit, his sophistication, his delight in word-play are constituent elements of his craft. Among some five hundred manuscripts submitted to the 1970 Yale competition, *Lugging Vegetables to Nantucket* is the only one, to the best of my recollection, that made me laugh, and perhaps in a sorry world that is as good a reason as any for being partial to it. Who else could have rewarded me with the little joke of the lady anthropologist, otherwise known as the dean of menopause: "But I have lost touch with the Touchwas"? I do not mean to suggest that this is a lighthearted poet. If one fails to catch the joke, one might as well shudder.

The gift for nonsense is one of the signs of the poetic character. Some of Peter Klappert's simplest inventions have the auditory smack of a child's counting-rhyme:

> Up in my attic I've got a bazooka
> That used to belong to Joe Palooka.

When Klappert takes aim at the human comedy, his "bazooka" transforms itself into a more complicated instrument of social satire, as in "The Babysitters," the central poem of his first collection:

> When I wriggled my big toe in under
> Her dichotomous athletic ass, she took off
> Ostrogoth's shoe and stroked his sole.
> When I ran my right hand under her jersey
> And tweaked her left breast, she ran her left hand
> Up his leg as far as the crotch. Loyal
> Faithfully watched.

In its offhand polymorphous way the passage exemplifies Klappert's impertinent assurance as a writer—some might call it his "nerve"—and his cool, almost allegorical, vivacity. An examination of "The Babysitters" may help to reveal the disciplines he works with and certain of his characteristic poetic strategies.

The poem's title alludes to the poet's friends, "who have seen me through these troublous times, who have indulged my weaknesses and returned kindness where I have been bitter, who have been my babysitter." The action occurs in the mind of the protagonist at a literary party, where the main preoccupation of the guests is with one-upmanship and sexual conquest. (The analogy, in a larger context, would be a concern for power and self-interest rather than for truth or beauty.) The different "voices" of the poem represent aspects of the speaker's personality. Sometimes he asserts his presence as a detached observer, sometimes as a resentful participant, sometimes as a self-pitying introspective sensitive plant; sometimes he lapses into free-association, and sometimes, as in his letters to Elsie, he attempts (generally without success) to be honest. The poem opens formally, with everything, it would seem, under reasonable control. As the situation gets out of hand, we experience a gradual process of disintegration, with both language and sentiment running down.

The seven sections of the poem, I am advised by the author, take their titles from "the Lasswell Formula," by which any communication is divided into seven elements: (1) who, (2) says what, (3) to whom, (4) under what circumstances, (5) by what means, (6) with what purpose, and (7) with what effect. The poem ends with the knowledge of the loss of Elsie and with an effort to live with that knowledge. Having failed to establish communication with others, the protagonist faces the necessity of reconciling himself to himself, of finding his place in the scheme of things.

Here as elsewhere one of the implications of Klappert's work, never directly stated, is that he must mediate between his sense of a poetic vocation and his other role as bemused guest at the festival of life, the higher nonsense of a dissolving universe. He must pass beyond the flippancy that permits him, or one of his voices, to say, "We are all caught up in a masquerade, / It's in moments like these that poets get made"; and he must search within himself for the grain of authentic feeling: "Elsie, I am so angry, and so lonely, and sorry about everything."

Another key work in the collection is the opening poem, "Pieces of the One and a Half Legged Man," a nightmarish vision, as powerful as it is outrageous, of the mutilated self, "Jesus Christ Remnant," sitting in the center of the world's zoo, suffering obscene indignities at the hands of others, vainly appealing for succor to the malign authority of The Court of Divine Justice, before which he must plead "filthy or not filthy."

> *"What were you looking for when*
> *the leg came off?"   "Looking*
> *for God, looking for the great totem."*
> *"How many totems have you found lately?"*

Even here a savage humor comes into play, as the merciless interrogation continues:

> "Have you ever loved?" (I
>   kissed her) "and what
>   was it like?"
>   (I kissed her).
> **She**
>   arched her heart
>   up from the mattress
>   and took the room
>   into her eyes:
>   "It was like
>   driving the car."

"Pieces of the One and a Half Legged Man" is more than simply ironic or satiric. It is one of the cruelest poems I know, a cleverly brutal phantasmagoria, swarming with images of the grotesque and ugly, and creating out of them a kind of triumph, a bravura spectacle of human entrapment. If there is an easy way out, the speaker's naked voice at the last does not pretend to have found it:

> I can betray you
> with no resolution; this is the metropolis
> and you are in danger here, but where will you go?

Peter Klappert's speech is natural and colloquial, though steeped in his literary information and sometimes deliberately salted with echoes, as in the Eliotish rhythms of the first movement of "The Babysitters." The search for a form is part of his poetic process, and when it suits his purpose he lets the process show or simulates its effect—for instance, in the canceled portions of his letters to Elsie. On the other hand, his poems are full of prosodic secrets. "Rowayton at 4 P.M." is based on the principle of alternating nine- and seven-syllable lines. "A Man I Knew" is essentially syllabic, but it conceals an internal, irregularly spaced Petrarchan rhyme scheme (strong, guest, request, belong, wrong, invest, rest, long, fence, table, block, sense, fable, locks). He is so confident of his ear and of his technical virtuosity that he does not hesitate to ring repeated changes on a rhyme or to build a towering pyramid of redundancies. In the breakdown phase of "The Babysitters" he alternates between semidoggerel and gross invective, of which he proves himself a master. When the burden of his voice is elegiac, he is capable of a broad, deep-channeled music that reaches back in time to a great tradition. I quote from his moving lines "In Memory of H. F.":

> Summer upon summer the Sound
> fell upon the mouthing river,
> striped bass and bluefish wandered
> among the rocks, weed creatures scavenged
> in the breakwater wash. Broad summers
> we have known the land would shift;
> we could not catch the momentary trembles
> but saw, on morning walks, sand fill

our footprints, and found new boulders
in the sea below the bluff. We know
of sea, that it breaks the whole world down,
or builds it, in some other sea.

Peter Klappert has made an elegant and bold beginning. Few poets of his age—or you may multiply his age—can equal him in his command of craft. He has a wicked eye, a nimble mind, audacity, and zest. Nothing fools him long, even his own postures. As he has written, *"Camera is a child-hood game, almost as fun as Doctor."*

Despite his taste for extravagances, he has too much existential awareness and too highly developed a critical faculty ever to settle for an ornamental art. "Melville," he observes, "knew the cost / of falling off the portico / into a design of hanging vines."

For a young man he has already disburdened himself of much of the gear and baggage of his adolescence, those guilts and hangups that make so many poets hobble for a lifetime. He is strong enough to contemplate the ultimate absurdity of being alive, and free enough to keep on searching for ancestors and meanings. At twenty-nine Klappert has already made a brilliant voyage and caught a vision of those hills on the islands where "men are raising broccoli, grapes, bayberries, beach plums, and lighting their lamps with whale oil." I wish for him that he will continue lugging vegetables to Nantucket.

Stanley Kunitz

I

PIECES OF THE ONE AND A HALF LEGGED MAN

I. Zoo

The one and a half legged man
in the triangle, eating his allegory,
is the ape at the Bronx Zoo who sits
with his legs before him, and his over-ripe
stomach before him, obscuring the fact;
is that ape, only pink like a suckling pig.
Only he doesn't finger his feces
or taste his own urine, only
(we gave him a heavy blue coat).
His lip hangs, it is a hung lip,
and his quick eyes speckle through the crowd
like doubt, picking into the sockets
of catacombs for the bright dark jungle.

> ... *I remember,*   *or someone has*
>   *told me*
>   *(there was something I wanted to*
>   *say, something to*
>   *look for, I   remember)*

The timid dreams
        flash into the forest
            and escape
though the dry grass
        whispers
                "necessary, necessary"
    and the mud-colored
            adder
                    answers "fear."

II. Kindergarten

If a man were born without legs
or lost them attempting totem, if
his arms were tucked in at the shoulders
and he carried his ears in a sack,
if we broke off his nose and twisted his tongue
with pliers, amputated an eye
and left his manhood intact
                              look, to hell
with the one and a half legged man.

The Funny Man in the triangle, eating
his heart, isn't a tripod.
The Little Boy will take his picture.
The Little Boy's Daddy is a Green Plymouth Stationwagon;
Mommy drives it to the Grand Union. They love
their Little Boy, and
he has been a Great Bargain to them.

   zip zip he-he-he-he-he
   (he laughs himself into the air.)

Camera is a childhood game, almost as fun as *Doctor*.

III. Smorgasbord

The soft tar sits in the road
but the hot rubber wives' tires screech.

Well, the pome
in the more-or-less-green in the triangle
swallows the allegory no hands;
he sucks the nutrients out of the atmosphere
and that has been a great surrogate to him.

EAT:

Greasy thick slices of Mrs. Fat Fat
with a garnish of parsley. Lunch time.
I will buy you the unction supreme:
amoeboid syrup on white ice cream.

It's two hundred degrees in the tar
and the streets have run into the sewer.
The sidewalk is sizzling white.
The sidewalk is sizzling white.
Sticktomesticktome said my undershirt
as I packaged me into the elevator
the sidewalk is sizzling white.

Hot, the tar is hot, and the sidewalk is sizzle.

Tell me sixty-six stories of cold concrete
and I will drink this julep to your Scarsdale plantation.

                      Have you forgotten
something? Forget something. Four hundred pounds
of tenderized meat doesn't beep
doesn't roll doesn't sizzle. See how it sits
with its eye open, and a lower lip.
Give him rose glasses and an overcoat: he has eaten
a bologna sandwich.
                      The landlady
fixed it for him
                      on the white enamel table in her kitchen.

IV. The Court of Divine Justice

He has a ticking in his soul, and prays;
his heart is infected with doubt, forgive him,
he has a ticking in his soul.

Will the remnant please
be carried forward:
Name? (look when you answer)
Objection, we are not interested
in the remnant's name
                    Oc-cupation?
Objection we are not and so forth but
Now Mr. Remnant, is it or is it not true/
you came here intending to sue/
Miss Thanwich Nograter who/
denied you the Power of Screw/ yes or no
what were you doing when the leg
came off? how do you *objection we are not* plead
filthy or not filthy? up on your stumps
yes or filthy the remnant must answer for himself
(speak up please)
            ORDER IN THE COURT
            REMNANT WANTS TO
anyone who speaks is a remnant for life
speak up on your stumps: what were you up to
when your tongue fell out *ShutUp!*

(. . . I created, or someone has told me)

                            it says here
ears remnant, pink pulpy *ears,* pendulant
succulent *ears,* ponderous preposterous *ears,*
swimming in ears, diving in ears, dreaming
of gallons of ears
                EARS?
                    Jesus Christ **Remnant**
what were you *doing?* (speak up please)

6

what was his job? triangle-sitter yes yes
but what does that mean? look remnant: what the hell
were you doing with all those ears? (face the jury)
(there is no jury) what kind of fantasy
life is that remnant? *trinity divinity unity infinity yes*
yes, but cut 'em into bacon strips I'd say. Catechism
remnant repeat after me: this man is a state of mind
this man is a state of mind (repeat after me after me)
Ears! Catechism remnant repeat after me: trinity is a delta
in the stream of traffic, trinity is a playground for scholars,
trinity is a pretty ring in the orchestrated chaos, trinity

"erase me"

Who mangled the monument remnant?

"erase me,
backward in time
Love   "

Stand up in your head remnant, I can't erase you.
You have swallowed the point-handed clock remnant,
feel it there ticking like a heart ticking
in your belly? tick-ing. Eat of the point-handed
ticking remnant, *I can't erase you.*
Good luck to those who can.

V. Eden

"What were you looking for when
the leg came off?" *"Looking*
for God, looking for the great totem."
"How many totems have you found lately?"

. . . . .

"Have you ever loved?" (I
kissed her) "and what
was it like?"

(I kissed her).

She
arched her heart
up from the mattress
and took the room
into her eyes:
"It was like

driving the car."

. . . . .

Come with me back to the park,
it is humble where the hunchback sits.
We will watch clumsy feathers
dance to the ground and delight
that the woodthrush disturbs them. We will
look how the ducks dos-a-dos.
I, too, have been looking for totem,
and my eyes are full for the consummation.
No. This is the acropolis and the forum;
we must bring our problems before it.
Weary of the mute priest,
weary of baiting the bull, of the cock-fight
and the prize-fight, thump of the glove
and cling of the steel talon

(if you have looked at a jack-hammer
you will know the strength of concrete)
the head pounds, but the carpeted house
is no buffer.
                Swallow the dog's mouth,
suited to tearing meat; take of the quilted fist,
the glove to the groin, the clawed throat,   and the park
is crowded on Sunday.
                I can betray you
with no resolution; this is the metropolis
and you are in danger here, but where will you go?

II

THE BABYSITTERS

*The way out is via the door, how is it
no one will use this method?*
—Confucius

WHO

When we sat in the high ceilinged room
I thought of geometric figures and wet
A new cigar. "Poetry is where we are."

Fire broke over the tiers of wood
We had carried in from the weather,
And we drank mulled cider out of refined
Desire to seem apropos and sparse.
Oh, we had love in its twisted colors
Binding us one to another, muscle
And mucous and venom, and perhaps some
Two dozen devices attempted before.
Cigarette smoke eddied in the patterns
Lanterned by the fire on the walls.

> *for hours as the sun passed it swam*
> *against the current, against the flotsam:*
> *in its head it had secret knowledge*

I was thinking of something else.

Elsie—

Ostrogoth, Miriam, Loyal and I,
And across the room a number of people
In love or represented by their wives.
They were weighing each other and spoke
Of nature and artifice; recondite
Allusions stamped their feet in the hall.
We four talked of each other in silence.

> *a lizard's tail twitching in the desert*

> *a bull-whip flicked out through the dark*

Elsie I've given you all and now I'm bluffing

> *the mortician's antebellum mansion*
> *on the Mississippi, his chandelier*
> *controlled by rheostat, the way he talked*
> *about his husbands*

Elsie the only love poem I've ever written November
14th 1967

> *the Pied Piper in Leder-hosen, a bull-whip*
> *in his back pocket*

I can't stand my own designs
Elsie when will the human war begin in earnest?

> *the way you said, "Your letter was perceptive*
> *but a bit late," and suggested I read*
> *a book by some psychiatrist*

Go fuck . . .
I don't feel good don't bother me
Elsie I'm serious

> *a boa constrictor, gagging*

We pegged together a seminar
With the short ends of pencils and dreams.
I said there were quite a few subjects
For poems; Ostrogoth said "There are Two."
Loyal swallowed a piece of cheese. "Ahl wahrs
Ahr sexhewahl wahrs."
                        (Ostro picked teeth
With a bone.) "All poetry is is war."
Digestion followed digestion, Miriam
Followed with mouthwash. "I see only
One subject for poems."
                        There was a reason
For our congestion, there was something
Gluing us together, but sticks of furniture
Furnished the room in which we lent ourselves
        to poetry.

14

Beauty and Poetry contain the same number
of letters, but Beauty requires all three
lines of a standard typewriter keyboard.
The typewriter, of course, has had great
impact on the form and content between which
there is no dichotomy in modern poetry.

>   *"Let's talk about*
>   *the poem as it stands on the page."*
>   *Lou brought two small ones—*

A further distinction is Instinct. Instinct
refers to unlearned, patterned, goal-directed
behavior which is species-specific.
Freaks you would say.

>   *two small ones which she wears high*
>   *where no one can miss them.*
>   *I should have been kind and noticed*
>   *but*

Nov. 14, 1967

Dear Elsie,

After one year without even a note I would like to tell
you a true thing. What I loved about you was the possibility
of love. Elsie, I've never even had a fantasy about you. I
feel like a stringed instinct and someone ignorant of music
is trying to play me . . .

Nov. 14, 1967

Dear Elsie,

~~Look don't condescend to *me* Elsie I was a prodigy my-
self once~~

15

Do I seem less stable since we stopped it? am I bitter?
I would like to write another love poem—that or be remem-
bered as one whose premature death deprived the world of
—Bitch! Say it: "Never use two words if one would be
superfluous. . ." Elsie give me a chord ~~which will ravel and~~

At this point big-bangers split
into two branches. One holds
the galaxies will continue to fly outward
forever, the other speculates
mutual attraction
will ultimately cause them to slow down,
stop, and fall back together
like a handful of pebbles
tossed into the air.

which will ravel and unravel me forever . . .

The male three-spined stickle-back,
a small fish, guards his nest.
He drives other males away, but
if a female approaches he courts her,
or he courts her egg-laden outline.
That's fine for the stickle-back.

> *Austin wants a subject large enough*
> *for his canvas; he wants a canvas*
> *large enough. But he is waiting*
> *for the shape to take hold*
> *and for the hole to take shape.*

(It's all right until you begin to suspect.
Then nothing satisfies
but the defense of your full scheme—
the three dots, the behavioral twitch,
the signal intended for the mate—
ruffled plumage and an abrupt jerk.
The response: a fat flutter of eye-lids,

16

a kiss, a cloacal kiss in mid-air.
And you watch it. You do not miss a muscle
or move one
      —Are you the ethologist with small binoculars?

The feathers are not quite right.
It must be the time of the year
or this particular light (late sun
through high branches) and so you wait;
certainly this is the freak you must
add to your list, the classified aberration,
deviant, pervert
      —Omniscient Ornithologist!

Freaks you would say. Can you speak
the language of bees? tell me the way
to the clover patch. There is a hum
as the sun passes, there is a great gathering
of cellophane and filaments,
a murderous heat, a humus,
a promiscuity among the weeds.
Did you make them? Were you there?
Can you control them?
      —You! Malignant Lepidopterist!

Nov. 14, 1967

Dear Elsie,
    Can you put out the moon with a pea-shooter? I'm walking on nobody's eggs, I'm as moral as I can remember. What if I were to call you William? What if I were to call you—Lassie?
    But if Lassie liked it, and I liked it . . .

Chink Chink says the Chaffinch
and a thousand chaffinches mob
the outline of an owl.
               Too bad
for the essential features of owlness.

17

TO WHOM

Enter mine host
With a sheaf of foundation grants
And a neatly pressed pants.
He is the social Eumenide,
Provider of these amenities.
We sit in his vacuous affair
His palace in the very air
We breathe
And we conceive
From his suggestions. Oh, *he was no forpynëd goost*
But the monk who keeps learning alive.
A fat goose lovëd he best
Or else a breast.

Our wives start stalking each other
They bristle and ripple their gristle.
Suddenly there's a crowd and sulky Yvette
Steals out of her Mexican shroud. She laughs
Out loud. And our condescending confucian
Focuses into a yawn: rebirth is reborn.

   (who had his ears in the clouds and failed to sleep
   who was a walking catatonic
   who carefully had not neglected to breathe
   who made up schedules of himself, who made up timetables,
     who stood in the rain and missed every bus

   who touched on the subject touching the subject
   who defined himself by the lighting around him
   who sat Monday morning in the bar without his glasses
     and memorized in the mirror the blurred face
     of the clock
   who started nothing—

who ate cashews who ate butternuts who ate peanuts who
   ate sunflower seeds
who suffered a partial eclipse
who was there, who saw what was coming (probably) and
   stayed where he was
who did what had to be done as if he hadn't heard the news
who woke up dying, who died
waking up. Who ran away with himself who ran . . .

Mine host does his introductions:
He conjures names with one hand, with the other
He opens a can of applause
                    —Outbursts of
Orchids emblossom and cascade
From the neck of America's finest champagne,
We are all caught up in a masquerade,
It's in moments like these that poets get made.

UNDER WHAT CIRCUMSTANCES

We breathe the same air. Twice.
A layer of ash suspended.

Where do the bacilli enter

where we dropped them from the dock
or where the current takes them?
They were pebbles, they were flagstones.

. . . . .

This is a phenomenon that stopped, this
is a bag of gears.
                    This simplicity is stone,
sea-water, air. A rotting dock.
We stood on the dock. We memorized the haze.

    Elsie, How does one come down from ecstasy? how does
one walk?
    Do you remember bringing the *Green Turtle* in after an
easy day on the Sound, how we yawed in the late, slow
swells, passing the reef between Sheffield Island and the
lighthouse, pushing the boom out, and that big foolish sail
out on a reach, coming in, coming home, watching the sun.
    Elsie how do I explain to you . . .

When Ostrogoth lies on his back
In his permanent slacks, he stretches
The length of the pallet. He speaks
An Indo-Frankish tongue, in a gentile manner
With Nordic feet, wears arrow shirts
And winged shoes, and likes to dance.
He does not smoke or drink or curse
(except in verse) and would like to be
Complete. He thinks he wants not to want

When he wants not to suffer. Miriam
Gives him a soft erection and says
It will soon be over. Someone else frowns.
But Miriam has been around, and she knows
Perfection is the perfect protection.
     Which moves us in our direction.
Miriam leans on my knees and is
Easy to please. She grows less soft
With each breaking dawn, but her needs
Are far between in an age of Art.
She wants a homo to come home to—bring
A friend home tonight—she wants
A prominence she cannot climb
Or plenty of time to herself.
She likes us all here on this pallet.
     Loyal is long and pale. He folds his bones
On a corner of the divan and wears
A tea-tray smile like a wilting boutonniere.
He sits in his appointed way and pulls
His left earlobe. Was he listening
For a clever play with words when I heard
Ostro say "I wish that famished O
Would blow away"?

                         11–14–67
Elsie why did you go home with ~~that shithead~~ Arnold stop
playing on my sympathy ~~you know~~ you don't need the prac-
tice. What am I going to do ~~with all this time~~ you've left
me ~~with~~?

    Do you know you have disrupted my life?

    Look, maybe I could call you while Arnold—I wouldn't
mind the embarrassing pauses—I have a book of dirty
pictures I could look at. Would it bother you—to know
I was reading *at a time like that?*

    Elsie I'm writing a long poem called the Lasswell
Formula.

    You could always put down the telephone . . .

Ostrogoth

Lies on his back in trifolium
Like nobody's lover. He is a kind
Of diagonal, bisecting a wrong triangle.
We are a tetrahedonist.

BY WHAT MEANS

When I wriggled my big toe in under
Her dichotomous athletic ass, she took off
Ostrogoth's shoe and stroked his sole.
When I ran my right hand under her jersey
And tweaked her left breast, she ran her left hand
Up his leg as far as the crotch. Loyal
Faithfully watched.
     The bird in the hearth
Turned to a uniform grey haze. Sticks of furniture
Littered the room . . .

   Well, we have commenced yachting.
   Loyal angles on one corner of the raft
   Reading a *Sailing Manual*.
   Before we get into shore
   He'll take graft in the aft.

   Ostrogoth squats on his heels
   And tries to talk really earnest
   To a poet named Lou—ambiguity's fool!
   But a stool is a better tool
   For working it out.

   & Whom is that watching Who? Miriam
   No doubt wonders about Lou's clothes
   But Miriam seldom blunders until
   She knows. Her sense of the line
   Has made her write prose before.

(You'd think by now these welts on my back
would have knitted, healed, flaked away,
that the pus would have dried, the sting melted
—the boils, abscesses, cysts, ecthyma, the scabrous
mange, the lacerations and burns from robes and whips,

the sprained metacarpals, the ragged ends of long fractures,
the eroded terrain, shrapnel wounds, leprous mottle, festering,
drooling tumors, cold dry gaseous humid inflammatory
progressive spontaneous fulminating oral traumatic
gangrenous malignancies!
they spread their webs like arachnids . . .

At this quiet crossroads, bucolic interlude, self-conscious
retreat, I would like to thank my friends who have seen me
through these troublous times, who have indulged my
weaknesses, and returned kindness where I have been bitter,
   who have been my baby-sitter.

> One hour out from shore
> And everyone's found a place.
> Miriam has a heart on
> And wears it with innocent Grace.
> Even Loyal is stuffing a mug
> With an empty caress
> —why, the passionate pilgrim
> himself has been making progress:
> Lou slobbers at Austin, Ostro
> rummages under Lou's dress.

Nov. 14, 1967

Dear Elsie,
   Elsie, why do they go about their lives as if nothing
happened? They go about and about their lives, they go
about and about and about their lives they go about. And
people pass in the alley below me. Male! and Female!
   ~~Elsie wouldn't they do better if they knew what their minds are about?~~ Elsie wouldn't we do better if

They can't get any help they haven't
   applied for it their tongues are
     kelp their lungs are full of
bat guano their brains are infested with

24

           spiders they corrupt the air itself with
               their bloody rectums they eat
the stomachs of shy animals and break
        the eggs of birds and burn
            the hovels our fathers wove
of leaves and twigs and hung with lichens and mosses their
bodies are green and rotten their bodies are
        falling from trees they have more faces than
            public clocks their urinals gurgle like
mouths their public breath brings Black Plague their public
        teeth are heavy with icebergs electricity rattles
        their
            eyes their cocks are poisonous
mushrooms their cunts are withered
        condoms their balls never descended their
        tits are going to explode THEY WILL PASS
        THROUGH THE PUBLIC HUMP OF A CAMEL!

WITH WHAT PURPOSE

The seven-toed Dodo is not so extinct
as you thinkd. It is commonly found
floating on grey weather in uncertain
backwaters, where it is, nevertheless,
due to the origin of speciousness,
survival of the fittedest,
and its resemblance to a bruised
and somewhat deflated beach-ball.
　　The Dodo lives on barnacles,
conch meat (pieces of snail shell
and cloudy glass have been found
in the gizzards of dissected birds)
and the worms it attracts
with the odor between its toes.
　　Dodos always carry ladders
and occasionally roost
in the branches of old established trees.
Since they are all near-sighted and tone-deaf
they can be heard on clear nights, snoring.
Roosting Dodos are protected by law.
They propagate through their ambiguous toes
and in the spring migrate
by walking in the same direction.

After listening to landscape poetry
I became curious about fresh air

> *One ineffectual lover*
> *Sits on a corner of the pallet.*
> *His smile is no cover.*
> *He'd rather wear a gown*
> *And do the town.*

26

but the avenues were unclean
with nitrogenous offal
and there were ammonia smells
in the corners of tenements

> *Now Ostrogoth is young and fair*
> *And all the world is in his hair;*
> *When in ten years he's old and gay*
> *He'll find his world has fallen away.*

I found it difficult to be
sentimental about deposits
of sediment

> *Little Miss Muffit decided*
> *To bluff it, but*

rust and saprophytic fungi

> *Little Tommy Tucker*

the red slag of the river

> *Didn't want to fuck her*

became difficult

wasps deposited eggs amid
the sweet vapors
of decaying oaks

> *Jack be nimble, Jack be quick,*
> *Or Jack be behumped by a candle stick*

gnats and swamp flies
gathered above the ponds—

in this terrain
all resources eroded

I would nail our conversation
to the wall
or walk out on it all
and leave the sound waves breathing.
Yes, in a moment I will be leaving.

what could I have intended?
in a broken, purulent land
to discover myself, mended

      Well, I should think it would
      change a man

    Elsie, this is the last letter I'm not going to send. Elsie there are some poets, not muscular, not iridescent, whose poems are not mobiles—and yet one returns to them as one returns to a rock above the sea, a resort in the off-season. One listens to them the way one talks to a confidant, listens as I would talk to you . . .

      to step on a land-mine

AND WITH WHAT EFFECT

Today I will find a rock
folded like the grim old men in orange ribbons.

> Damn it Elsie! no poetry is war.
> Elsie, I think the mud is red now, and hot with the men
> who dived too far down. Nothing, not even buttons remain
> . . . Elsie . . . I am no doctor . . . have taken no oath . . .
> I cannot save any man's life.

Today I will find a formula
thick with an unbroken language
muttered in an unrepeatable tongue, composed
and recomposed like molecules strung out
and wrapped inside themselves.

> And our poets have—none of them dived down to that
> *black* red, that *black* laced with new mud, that *green,* that
> *black* cellophane palm spreading its *green* digits in a *vicious*
> design . . .

I will bask in the spotted sun.
It will be a high, hot day, and the breeze
will come in broken sequence, will be gaps
in a broken sequence, and the rock
will be full of faces, swaying.

> Elsie our poets are waiting for something that does not
> wait, for the idea of a beginning, a fine hair.
> And I have come this far to discover you were impatient
> and left without me.

And today the rock will sway
with the wasted faces and the high, hot breeze.
It will move as it moves at night.
We will crush follicles of grass,
centipedes, ant larvae, bayberry twigs,
we will drag them with us and they will sway
as the rock sways for the spotted sun.

Elsie, I am so angry, and so lonely, and sorry about everything.

LUGGING VEGETABLES TO NANTUCKET

A MAN I KNEW

So you have built your house strong
yourself, and no one comes in
but knocks, and comes in as a guest.
And you no longer desire
to request anything beyond
this land, which belongs to you.
Oh, you are right, that you were
wrong to borrow and rent and
not invest in something of
your own. For the rest, one's
neighbors are the world and life
is long.
       Or that is your view
as you sit behind your fence,
behind your lawn, window and
table. One comprehends so
little of the block beyond
one's block, and one has such an
understanding with one's self,
that it is only common
sense not to credit fables,
to order groceries by
telephone, and mind the locks.

ROWAYTON AT 4 P.M.

For Ann Ford

She sits in the expanse the sun leaves
when its wake has parted
and run on into the afternoon

and thinks of the calm which burns off
before the sun is well up.
After the morning flood of light comes

this ebb and dryness, rocks and mudflats
emerging within the cove,
patches of brown among brown-green,

colors stirring in a slack breeze.
If she were offshore
she would let the sails luff and her boat

go aground. With the tide and wind coming in,
she would run before them
wing and wing, and leaving the islands behind,

be home when the traffic begins, when her boys
trail up from the beach
and her husband arrives on the 5:14.

ON A BEACH IN SOUTHERN CONNECTICUT

Gradually the monotony of his rhythms
overwhelmed him, like the repetition of small waves
on a beach in southern Connecticut.
This had been good, a good; but moderation
in excess, even the moderate luxury
of a rocky coast, became, finally,
one lesson in the same, old discipline:
excess leading to wisdom, and what good is wisdom?

The circles superimposed themselves, the sun
superimposed itself, on the same spot,
in the same sky, the same, in all practicality,
over the same beach. It was monotonous here
and good; the tempo of the sun was a familiar
tempo, but not a song to dance to.

Any change was needed. Almost any change.
Pacification of the prairie land-wars,
forgetting the skirmishes of cattlemen
and sheepmen, and the insomniac coyote,
had been effected on a furlough by the sea,
a truce. War and a truce were the first lessons:
not variations on a theme, but
alternation of all the possible routines.

If only the sun would bloom again with blood
he might intone a song with consonance.
Or if it shrivelled into haggling
inconsequence—as on a muggy day
a gullish cacophony composes
a rhapsody, for nerves teased into sympathy.

If only he could bring himself to sacrifice
this peace to all that chintz. Of course, to be
truly satisfied would be to forget
one's disaffections, would be to forget
the cult of satisfactions is a cult
and to forget one had forgotten. To forget
to anticipate. To be caught up
in an expanding and contracting

—hunger. He had forgotten lunch
and now it must be nearly half-past four.
Gin and bitters: crackers, triscuit, sea biscuit:
gouda, port salut, cheddar: braunschweiger:
anchovies or smoked mussels: and then dinner.
The old critique of heaven: no hunger. No stomach ache.
    No wisdom. Nothing.

IN MEMORY OF H. F.

d. Man of War Key, March 1, 1965

I found the land above the river, where
the river meets the sea, fallen off
into the Sound
            Ann writes to me, Hobey,
that you have drowned in your own years.

There was no fault in the massed earth,
nor was there in the sea. The fault
fell at birth, and whatever rooted
in the broken land—cedars, rockwart,
or the great and other sea birds:
dependent creatures, nested in the bluff—
knew it was there, and loved
the hollow where the sea resounded.

Summer upon summer the Sound
fell upon the mouthing river,
striped bass and bluefish wandered
among the rocks, weed creatures scavenged
in the breakwater wash. Broad summers
we have known the land would shift;
we could not catch the momentary trembles
but saw, on morning walks, sand fill
our footprints, and found new boulders
in the sea below the bluff. We know
of sea, that it breaks the whole world down,
or builds it, in some other sea.

Friday . . . cedars, terns, crustaceans.
but as if a part of the land mass had fallen,
it is quiet as the sun rises above the Sound.

37

POEM FOR L. C.

I. I have only the sound of your steps
   to guide me in this wilderness.
         (Tagore, "The Cycle of Spring")

Honey-suckle, nightshade,
the burdock tree; the hawthorn,
the spiney hawthorn with hand branches
and rock bound roots. Mud.

Protect your face. Know how to
recognize flowers, even in gardens,
know the medicinal herbs,
sweet and rude, though they be tame.
Tread paths with dry feet, leave
careful footprints. Lead me, and follow.

I have seen these thickets before
though the meadow escapes me;
don't let them tear at your eyes,
don't look back at me now, no more
than a glance. I am lost
as you are, I am tired,
I am making a home of this wood.

Buttercup, columbine, borage,
ash green thyme of the mint family.
Remember them. The weather has not been mild
and will not be mild tonight;
tomorrow, or over that hill,
look back if you can. Frail flowers
tenacious as weeds, have mystical powers.

Love me. Show by the path you tread
you love me now. Tomorrow,
or over that hill, look back if you can.

*II. Nothing is competent nothing is
all there is.*

(Creeley, "The Immoral Proposition")

I have brought you the wrong way, and I'm sorry.
The path you wanted is back, out of the thickets
of rhetoric; follow the trampled plants.
Metaphor began with words, and metaphor

misleads: 'buttercup' and 'columbine' are weeds,
they have no healing powers. Shallows of color,
texture and euphony make no flowers last.
The inscriptions of hawthorns cling.

And there is no truth beyond logic—surely
you have walked in circles looking.
Meadows grow into forests, and wilderness
clearings erode or strangle in neglect.

Perhaps there was a valley, and a path,
though this path ended. 'Love' is a conceit
earned in commitment; we are unintentional
liars. My figure has led you to briars.

THE LOCUST TREES

The stanchions leaned open and a faint
phosphate dust drifted in the barn
as we set out across the acreage
drawing and stapling as we went.
By evening, when the cows waited
to be led through the pasture gate,
a ductile web embraced the locusts
weathering against Culver's north ridge.

The fence stretched taut through the months
of seeding and spraying.
     In August
when the first cutting had been baled
and mowed, the one inch staples had bitten
well into the trunks of the locusts
and a thin cork crept over the wire.
The trees' roots groped in the soil. The fence
began to put out leaves and leafy twigs.

We were hauling stones and pouring
concrete for the new milk house, when John Culver
sprained his back, but the men from Dover
continued work on the glass pipeline.
Steam, rising from the ensilage, mixed
with smells of grain and molasses
as we forked corn and broke bales of hay
to the rows of Holstein faces.

Rust from the fence leached upward
in the veins of the locusts, until
the trees, at last, are like trees
grafted to a metal fence. Their leaves
turn rust color and do not fall;
their branches bud with small thorns.

                              All winter
the trees and their tenacious vines have wound
together. An orange blaze tears the air.

GROTESQUE WITH A CHAGALL GOAT

I forced the pheasants' eyes until
they burst in the hot solarium.
What was left, later, was spaghetti
stuck in a pan, a handful of wet hair.
I stored them in a cold cellar.

Those small compulsive ants
lick the sappy membranes from the buds
on the peonies. They click their tongues
like a man with mechanical knees.
A white fungus performs on the lawn.

Slivers of thick green, onions, husks,
red sparks in a white corolla,
crocuses,then a rotary mower.
Daffodils like yellow cups and saucers
—brittle dreams need a brittle glue.
But if aphids get into the roses
I will dust them, with a fatal talc.

FOUR X-LOVE POEMS

got a wheel-barrow
plenty of sorrow

I. Memory Is a Positive Act

It may have been a waste of time
from here, to go back through
and hear myself confess that I

am an ex-florist, to harangue
myself in the greenhouse, to hear
the echoes that would have been there,

to prune and prune and pick
the slivered glass, witness
the execution of an act of love,

sweep together one last confusion
of orchids, and take them for myself.

II. *Come Home! Come Home!*

So much for the holiday.
Wrap the snow up in snow
and put it away. Scrape

the bones down to the bone.
Take a plane home.
Remember to see what

you saw. Having said what you
had to say, make a return
out of staying away.

III. *Morpheus, My Roommate*

In heat so thick you can fuck it
bald faces of lovers come swelling
and blossoming back. Hog-white
they erupt from black water and float
on a loitering musk. Great ferns
converse by the sea. Hyla frogs croon.
Swamp water laps at the moon.

Up through the difficult grasses,
through the skulls of old Plymouths,
on the breath of the poisonous river,
under the trestle, down by the depot,
in the streets of this sweaty town,
when every sign in the road
is a twelve-year-old girl or a cop—

*Do not look at me like a tired
remorseful mother, like a list
of errands to run. I have come here
to remember, come as a junkman,
a tramp with a wheel-barrow.*

*Summer rain, summer rain,
I have come to drain the marshes.*

IV. For His Friends Who Would Take Away His Wounds

he has nothing. No suggestions
and no desire to be rude.
One bubble must echo like another,
books may be nothing more than trouble.

Bring, if you will, Eidel-weiss
and mechanical clocks. Bring
copper bottom-paint, corks, and
an ointment for sunburn. Bring the long hairs
from shrunken heads and the safes
from sunken ships.
Bring Ganges water, and the people
suspended in it; bring belly-buttons
which are the last to burn.
                                        Icons intact
or in panels, Saint\Sebastian
full of pins and Saint Thomas
full of fractured light,
dark ages and enlightened ages,
a cyclotron and a scarab,
something red to chew
and something to smear on the forehead.
Mirrors and beads and hatchets
which double as peace-pipes.
                                        Bring a knife
strong enough for this knot
or bring a stronger disease.
Bring a cenotaph rearing
on its hind legs, an epigraph
and a paragraph of good prose.
Bring me a change of clothes.

But Christ don't bring more books.
They're not my cameo ring, not
my pipe and slippers, not my mid-night meal
of melba toast and kippers. No books
are full of hungry Psychotherapy,
and Therapy has sold herself to Butchery.
They lead the world in plumbing and anatomy,
they lead the world, they're part of a conspiracy.
You have yourselves to blame for this skulduggery;
I do not ask for help I ask for quackery.
I ask, my friends, to have another daiquiri.

FOR THE POET WHO SAID POETS ARE STRUCK
BY LIGHTNING ONLY TWO OR THREE TIMES

One is so seldom struck by
lightning, so seldom struck by
everything beautiful.

Oh, sometimes a butane fuel
truck intercepts you enroute
to a new supermarket;
if you even get a toot
out of that, you're lucky
to find a place to park it.

Or some guy stops, his car key
still plugged in his ignition,
hits you with a tire iron
(not even a fire arm) and
—what kind of inspiration
is that?

      And the impression
I get on occasions when
I am struck by the sidewalk
is something I will not talk
about. How pedestrian
can you get. (Though each upset
makes me considerably more
concrete than I was before.)

ELLIE MAE LEAVES IN A HURRY

There's some who say she put death up her dress
and some who say they saw her pour it down.
It's not the sort of thing you want to press

so we just assumed she planned on leaving town
and gave her money for the first express.
She had some family up in Puget Sound.

Well we are married men. We've got interests.
You can't take children out like cats to drown.
It's not the sort of thing you want to press.

We didn't know she'd go and pour death down,
though most of us had heard of her distress.
We just assumed she planned on leaving town.

There's some of us who put death up her dress
but she had family up in Puget Sound.
We gave her money for the first express.

Well we are married men. We've got interests.
Though most of us had heard of her distress.
You can't take children out like cats to drown,
it's just the sort of news that gets around.

49

THANKSGIVING

What a day to dismantle a roller-coaster.
Well, they are taking it down—
the tracks are all over the ground
and the ties drawn up. The ticket office
is shut, the calliope covered with tarps.

These workmen move their rides
from town to town, with the weather,
and a day gained dismantling
is a day to them. They are grateful
for the day gained, and for the silence
in a park where only ducks and I remain.

As if against the numb, fall sky,
sounds of hammers and crowbars,
and the changing voice of one man's oldest son,
rebound from pond to lightpole and away.
Tomorrow they'll be on their way
to Arkansas, or a place they haven't
been before; today they're making time.

Today they're making time. The doors
of the van are open, the van is dark.
The cars stand there in a line, as if
they are not well or have something
to tell the man who stands on the tail-gate.
This corner of the park is nearly flat.

SUICIDE

it is a complete confession of failure
the empty conch shell
in a tidal creek
      the small fish caught in an eddy
everything going backwards
insomnia
love rotting
      somewhere behind a log in the forest
it is the center of every circumference
the final point
idiot dot
      the enamel worn off the sink
it is nothing swallowing its mouth

MAIL AT YOUR NEW ADDRESS

I.

Did your car get you to Florida?
I know you don't like me
to say so but Mrs. Wilson says
the same thing. Please tell me
(collegt) if you are all
there. I hope you do not
sleep or do anything on the road.
In Georgia.
       Your father
should see all the leaves.
Walter has not raked
a girlfriend up the street and wont
rake anymore. Watch out or
theyll have the same thing Mrs. Wilson
says the friend stayed and look
what happened at Cornell?
                Even if you changed
college is no reason to come home.
But get a haircut. I know
the dean doesn't like you
to look like a gardener.

II.

There have been so many deaths
due to carbon m. poisoning
that this is just
a note to suggest you leave
a little air come into your room. Also,

I hope you don't get involved
with young men or older
or made from popies (?) and Hippy's.
I hope you are not letting the drugs
get you. And don't get mixed up
with drugs. It might spoil your change
for getting the cert. you are working for.
Remember, it is costing quite a lot.

Don't scold. I am afraid of your
trips to and near Chicago.

INSTRUCTIONS FROM THE DEAN OF MENOPAUSE

In this pleasant sitting I am pleased
to welcome you to what we hope

a very pleasant
years. Please try to think of me

your older sister
your mother
                    in Stilwell Hall.

Last year we had a little joke
a small minority
referred to me

The Tank. Please think of me

Your Mother. In my position
one tries to keep a sense of
balance.
                    I hear many voices

arguing
the air.

Credentials hang from my walls—25
yrs—field work—Amazon—anthropologist.

But I have lost touch with the Touchwas.

A little joke. A small minority
of posters. Credentials hang
from my belt

& keep the natives friendly.
The files are somewhere else.

Some few of you no doubt are reliable.
I hear voices. A small minority
hang from my belt.
                    One tries

you can't corner

a little joke

a tank.

            Study hard. Be neat.
Don't believe the rumors. Obey
the parking regulations,
                          be in the dorm
and study hard.

Perhaps Rousseau was wrong.
Perhaps Thoreau was wrong. You can't
corner all the rumors.
                    Obey, keep clean.

I *am* pleased.
Some few of you are reliable.
If you see something ugly, run it over.

SOME PEOPLE ARE NEVER SATISFIED

Perennial gardens drift about these walls,
jasmine and wisteria
now obscure the colonnades
—the often broken walks and ravaged arbors
where lovers came to talk
of what was heavier than thought.

Plato knew the price of pure belief,
knew the only antidote for poison
was in the margin.
                        Melville knew the cost
of falling off the portico
into a design of hanging vines.

Old echoes in the halls invite
the vandals in, but vandals
like ourselves can keep them out,
at least, by keeping from the gardens
where they lie.
                        And nothing else?

Stevens was unfair to Plato
as Plato would have been unfair to him.
And he shunned peripheral gardens
Melville loved and feared. Some hedges
Stevens sculpted are still here.

We've heard all this and more.
The leaves that muffle what you say
can be clipped and hauled away.

SKROPHODUPOLOS HONORED BY RECEPTION

She aches enthusiasm,
eats the navels of oranges.
He wears bourbon like a cologne. She asks

Are you in the Mind-Workers' Union?
He says *I carry my head
in this helmet for protection.*

So she begins again, after a moment
of silents. *A B-52 is a plane
not a form you fill out.* He leans to her

with the hands of a man who drinks too much—
*Up in my attic I've got a bazooka
That used to belong to Joe Palooka.*

She fingers a figurine. Then they ascend
to another level and she returns
a damaged child. Or he dies

of immaturity and collapses
into a pile of sleep.
                    Virtue
is not in not doing but in

not desiring to do & better to do
to no end than do nothing &
besides no armor can defend

a fearful heart: it kills itself within.

NO TURTLES

For ten months now
no turtles.

Walnuts.   Clumped
like mudballs on the rug.

I've done my best.
Washed the dishes, folded up
my clothes,

even swept the porch.   No
turtles
        blooming
in the turtle trees.

Softly, at night,
I hear the walnuts breathe,
but get down on my knees
or not

       no turtle movements
interrupt my sleep.

IOWA

A life of bottles by the kitchen sink,
lidless mornings sponging up the sun,
night letters in laundromats, afternoons
in watery cafes crouched against the wind.

My images are eating in the east,
dishes growing mold, growing empty,
clean as bone. Mind is what we gum it with
while love comes walking slowly from the west.

THE DRAWER

My grandmother says
                    something, but
the sounds are too weak
or too tired to climb the stairs
and so she begins again after
the first two steps.

                Something
is caught in the drawer and I
can't get it out.   Since it must be
something she needs, I get up
and go down to the kitchen.

The drawer can be opened by asking
What is it you need?
The drawer which has always been jammed.

DOSTOEVSKY SAID MAN

I.

Dostoevsky said man
is unhappy because he doesn't know

he is happy. What I am is
so real it dies on my lips.

II.

If I loved you I
would say no if you loved

me you would not let me
say it.

III.

Everything you say is cruel
and bitter glory in my mouth.

IV.

There is no disease for this cure.
I tell you what is

on my lips and what I know
it is too soon to know but

something is
falling from me like rain in sunlight.

PHOTOGRAPHS OF OGUNQUIT

Abbot Lot came to Abbot Joseph and said: Father, according as I am able, I keep my little rule, and my little fast, my prayer, meditation and contemplative silence; and according as I am able I strive to cleanse my heart of thoughts: now what more should I do? The elder rose up in reply and stretched out his hands to heaven, and his fingers became like ten lamps of fire. He said: why not be totally changed into fire?
(The Wisdom of the Desert, *translated by Thomas Merton*)

I.

On the last day you would not
let me take your picture. The sun
was shattering on glass,
the stonewharf hurt my eyes. I was angry
and the sky would not cloud over.

You were only twenty. It was the beginning
of the last day. The fishermen
refused to see the air between us,
the full face of your smile, the full
mouth, spitting. They sat eyeing the sea.

The wind ignited your hair. I resisted
your flight and walked away
way down the beach. The beach was full
of families. Your eyes were bluegreen.
Your distress was wild and anonymous.

I resisted your flight, now what more
must I do? The rocks hurt my eyes.
I was angry. I turned. The beach
was full of families. The fishermen
looked at their lines. Children are singing.

62

II.

The curtains stood up and watched us,
the swollen door was forced shut, we were
warped against each other. I could not
tell you from the humid air. I wanted
to say I will not want to take your
picture to tell the truth I wanted to say
the sheets are smothering I
wanted to refuse to sleep against
the door I wanted to say the room
is standing in the corners holding its breath.
When it was over, neither of us laughed.

III.

It was one o'clock. I'm not sure
how far I walked. You walked the wharf.
We walked back.

What you've given you cannot take
out of my hands, and what I've
given is still mine to give.
I take it with me, there is sand
in the shutter. Perhaps you meant
to leave it on the chair.

                    We will fight back
with anger and recriminations,
with demands and ultimatums.
The camera is set on #4. The fishermen
saw nothing.
            I hope the bus has brought you
safely to yourself.
                When you wouldn't pose
you said "Now what more must I do?"
Children were singing.

            The camera
        is at the bottom of the suitcase.

THE INVENTION OF THE TELEPHONE

The time it took he could have
crawled—on the hairs of his knuckles,
on his eyelids, on his teeth.

He could have chewed his way.
In a place without friction
he could have re-invented the wheel.

But he wanted you to be
proud of him, so he invented
the telephone before he called.

LUGGING VEGETABLES TO NANTUCKET

'One doesn't get married to broccoli'

I. Manhattan

But then, Ephebe,
broccoli isn't the whale hunt
and Melville is never dull.
I'm talking about tradition.
Broccoli isn't eggs frying
or a fertile yolk. I'm not talking
about eggs, I'm talking to you—
take your clothes off, forever.

The difference between broccoli
and spermacoeti is ripeness.
The analogy does not hold, is always
misleading. You, halver of pears,
composer of hemispheres, vestige
of Aristotle, know not even broccoli,
however it scatters its seed,
is married to broccoli. The distinctions
are mortal and eternal, constant
and inconsistent. Nothing can come
of a closed circuit, a short circuit;
nothing can come of that.

The broccoli is all in one bag,
the bachelors are all vegetable.
The married bachelors are all in one bag,
say inorganic, or animal.
Stones, perhaps. They are not the same,
that is the only difference.

II. Block Island

You said you trusted me and so
I edged through the crowded smoke
and came to old friends in the inferno

and trusted you. George and Larry
said something.   *—I can't hear you
in this red noise!*

                    If control is a color
control must be white. I remember
a theory of light . . .
                    One is intimidated
by darkness, but Blake would understand
the unpredictable has a place
in the totally predictable room.
What do *these* have to do with me?
Blue! Blue! And the wrong end of the bottle!

Can I find out what I would seek,
can I pass through the neck of time?   *—Oh,
distrust the sybil in the first two syllables,
she has black feathers and a red, red mouth.*

                    These ideas are mine
because I can say them:

   i. Marriage is a journey
      through eternity, passing a vortex
      unspoken, unspeakable.

  ii. Broccoli tastes better to a man on a
         whale hunt.

Why don't we go get a cup of coffee?
Why can't we go somewhere and talk about
        dichotomies?
Where are you?

 iii. Trust. Or the other solution—

III. Nantucket

Here is an endless expanse, here
is the ruminating ocean.

Out of sight of land, out of
the pressure of that atmosphere,
nothing is visible in the mind
but this forty-year-old yacht.
Failure of the imagination,
short circuit. And then, suddenly,

you are on the yacht with me,
although not controlled.
"How simple the solution to my problem is;
it needs simply not to be."
You are unpredictable, and I can
understand that.

            The crowded smoke lifts

    —LAND HO!

            On the hills of these islands
men are raising broccoli, grapes, bayberries,
    beach plums,
and lighting their lamps with whale oil.